Dogs Wanna Have Fun

Emilie Bilokur

Good Life Collections

Published by Good Life Collections.

Dogs Wanna Have Fun / Emilie Bilokur.
1. Adult coloring books.   2. Dogs.   3. Pets.   4. Stress reduction.
ISBN-13: 978-0692631300
ISBN-10: 0692631305

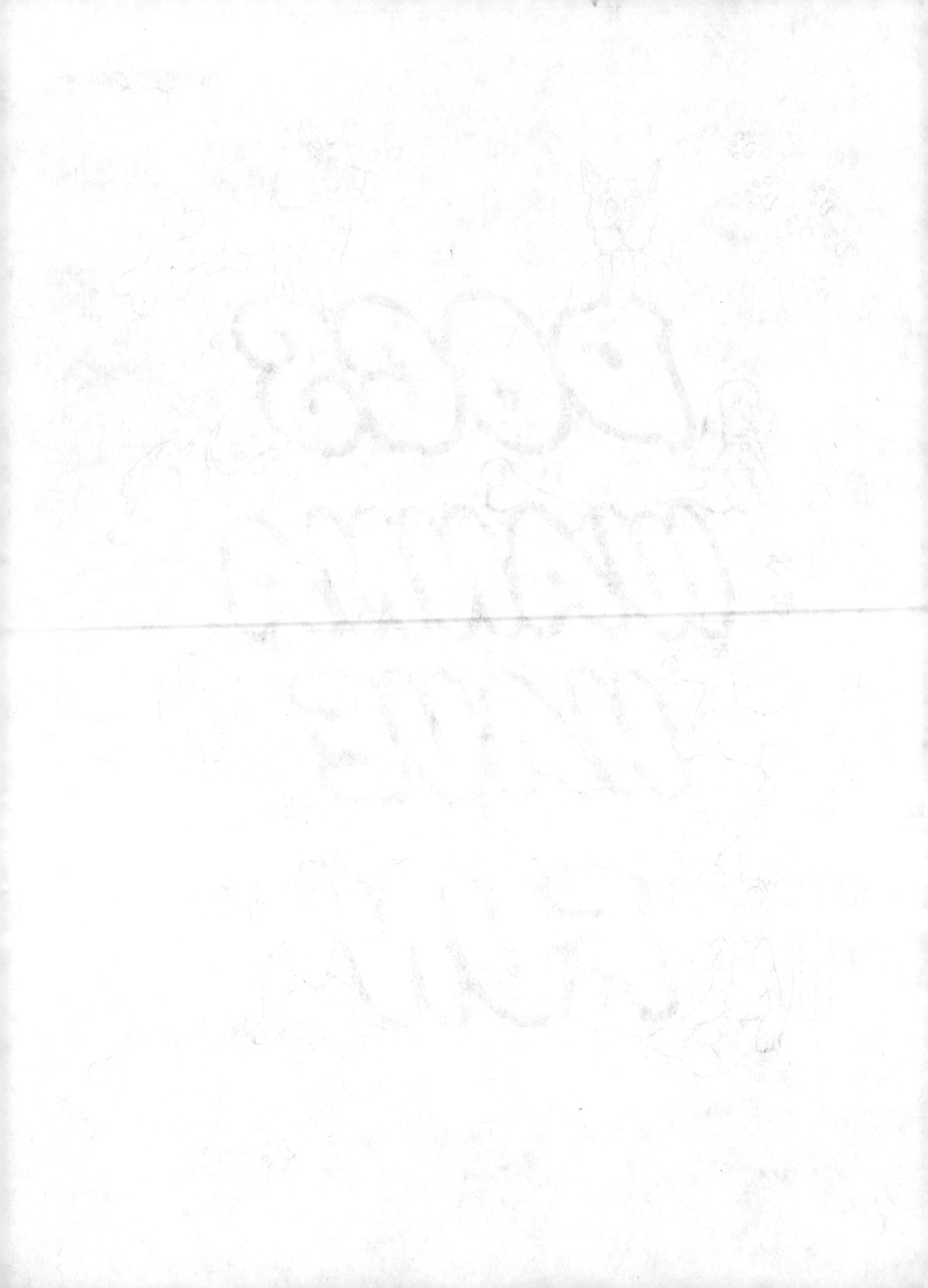

Welcome to your Coloring Journey!

I have a passion for coloring. Even before I went to art school, I bought and hid away coloring books of all types. I loved to color in them, but did it in secret.

There was just something about bringing colors together on a page that made me come alive in a way that nothing else did. I still have many of those coloring books, but now I have brought them out of the closet.

Today, since the art therapy movement, coloring has risen wildly in popularity. Folks have discovered that coloring reduces stress, lifts your mood and relaxes you in an almost magical way.

Coloring captures the attention of both sides of your brain. Your subconscious mind takes over, and you're the closest to the real you that you've probably been in a long time.

Feeling uncertain about which colors to use? Remember, you did this when you were four years old, and you were wonderful at it. Use the colors you like. You will quickly find your groove again, and soon you'll be saying "I did this? This is great!"

Here, this is your book now. I've expressed myself. Now it's YOUR turn to express yourself, and bring your own Color Magic to this black and white world.

Have a magical journey.

My best coloring tips (and some things to help you experiment with color):

1. Place a piece of paper or card stock under the page you are coloring, just in case the color bleeds through. The card stock will also add a 'cushion'.

2. There is no right way to color a picture. And there is no wrong way. Don't let anyone tell you different. Trust your instincts. Try color combinations and techniques that you like. To warm up, draw test strokes on blank paper. The book printer often adds blank pages to the back of a book; you may use them for this purpose.

3. If you are not familiar with color theory, here's an easy guide to mixing colors. Primary colors are yellow, blue and red; you can't get them by mixing any other colors.
If you mix any two of these primary colors, you will get the secondary colors of green, purple and orange.
If you mix one primary and one secondary color, you will get tertiary colors. Give it a try – mix and create!

4. You might start with inexpensive coloring tools if you prefer. Before long, you will probably find that you want to buy the best quality tools you can afford. They are well worth it, and will still be giving you a more gratifying experience long after the higher price is forgotten.

5. Forget rules. Do what you like and something unique will happen.

My favorite coloring tools:

Fiskars 48 Gel Pens (won't bleed through the page like many markers will)

Prismacolor Colored Pencils – thick lead and thin lead

Copic Ciao Art Markers – expensive but they color like a dream

Sakura Gelly Roll Gel Pens – a higher quality gel pen, expensive but delightful